Conference Proceedings
18 June 1999

TEACHING INTELLIGENCE
AT
COLLEGES AND UNIVERSITIES

Lloyd Salvetti, Director of the Center for the Study of Intelligence; LTG Samuel V. Wilson, USA (Ret.), President of Hampden-Sydney College and former Director, Defense Intelligence Agency; A. Denis Clift, President of the Joint Military Intelligence College.

CONTENTS

Program.   v

Remarks of Welcome, A. Denis Clift   1

Keynote Address, LTG Samuel V. Wilson, USA (Ret.)   2

Biography of General Wilson   10

Teaching Intelligence: Working Together to Build a Discipline,

   Lloyd Salvetti   12

Biography of Mr. Lloyd Salvetti   25

Closing Remarks, Dr. Ronald D. Garst.   27

Joint Military Intelligence College
Conference on Teaching Intelligence Studies at
Colleges and Universities

Friday, 18 June 1999

Defense Intelligence Analysis Center, Tighe Auditorium

CONFERENCE PROGRAM

0700-0830 Registration	DIAC Lobby
0830-0845 Welcome	A. Denis Clift, President, JMIC
0845-0930 Address	LTG Samuel V. Wilson, U.S. Army (Ret.), President, Hampden-Sydney College; Introduction by CPT Matthew Goodrich, JMIC
0930-0945 Break	Refreshments
0945-1145 Presentation of Papers	Moderator: Thomas Fields, JMIC
	Mr. Mark Marshall, JMIC, "Teaching Vision"
	Dr. Katherine Shelfer, Drexel University, "Structure and Core Competencies of the Drexel University Competitive Intelligence Certification Program"
	Dr. Mark Lowenthal, Open Source Solutions (USA), Discussant
1145-1300 No-Host Luncheon	Conference Attendee Reserved Seating Available in the DIAC Dining Room
1300-1345 Address	Mr. Lloyd Salvetti, Director, Center for the Study of Intelligence, CIA; Introduction by Ann Toll, JMIC
1345-1400 Break	Refreshments
1400-1500 Presentation of Paper	Moderator: Robert Mirabello, JMIC
	Dr. Davis Bobrow and Michael Rattie, University of Pittsburgh, "Outsiders and Outside Information: Toward Systematic Assessment"
	Dr. H. Bradford Westerfield, Yale University, Discussant
1500-1515	Refreshments

1515-1630 Presentation of Paper	Dr. Perry L. Pickert, JMIC, with Ms. Lilia Vazquez, UN Secretariat, David Traystman, U.S. Mission to the UN, and LtCol Peter Vercruysse (USMC), Joint Warfighting Center, "A Virtual UN Security Council: Educating for Multilateral Strategic Decisionmaking" Dr. H. Bradford Westerfield, Discussant
1630-1640 Closing Remarks	Dr. Ronald Garst, Provost, JMIC
1640-1800 Reception	DIA Patio

REMARKS OF WELCOME

"Teaching of Intelligence Conference"
18 June 1999

A. DENIS CLIFT
President
Joint Military Intelligence College

"Had I been present at the creation I would have given some useful hints for the better ordering of the universe." Dean Acheson borrowed from these words of Alfonso X the Learned, King of Spain, for the title of his post-World War II State Department memoirs, *Present at the Creation*. Sherman Kent, one of the Intelligence Community's founding fathers, might well have chosen that title for his 1949 Princeton University Press opus, *Strategic Intelligence for American World Policy*.

"Intelligence work," Kent wrote, "remains the simple, natural endeavor to get the sort of knowledge upon which a successful course of action can be rested. And strategic intelligence," he wrote, "we might call the knowledge upon which our nation's foreign relations, in war and peace, must rest."

The teaching of intelligence flows from such scholarship as it flows from more precisely defined research, historical examination, and from assessments and explorations of avenues for future advancement. We are honored to have among the scholars and practitioners with us this morning pre-eminent teachers and leaders in the field, Dr. Anthony Oettinger of Harvard University and Dr. Bradford Westerfield of Yale University, members of the Joint Military Intelligence College's Board of Visitors.

We welcome you. We welcome all in attendance this morning from colleges and universities across the United States, from the intelligence and national security communities, from the media, and from other nations in this hemisphere and overseas. We welcome the authors of the papers published in *A Flourishing Craft: Teaching Intelligence Studies*, which each of you has in your conference folder.

The teaching of intelligence at growing numbers of our colleges and universities — the teaching of its place, structure and practice in our democracy — offers the welcome prospect that growing numbers of young Americans will become attracted to the field. It offers the prospect that, increasingly, the very best of the coming generation's talents and capabilities will participate in the contributions of intelligence to the survival, security and well-being of the Nation. Indeed — if you will bear with a parochial aside — that once in the field, we will have occasion to welcome them to their professional, graduate studies at this college.

Today's program, and the conference papers available to you as contributions to the program, will give us a look at where the teaching of intelligence is today and where it is tending in the future. The product from today's presentations and discussions, the proceedings flowing from this work, should increase our understanding of how better to nurture this phenomenon so as to bring the very finest young American men and women into the intelligence ranks — national, theater and tactical — in the years ahead.

KEYNOTE ADDRESS

LTG Samuel V. Wilson USA (Ret.)
President, Hampden-Sydney College and
Former Director, Defense Intelligence Agency

INTRODUCTION

At the outset, I would like seriously to salute the aims of this conference. It is a good thing you do, for many reasons. For one, never has sound, responsive and timely intelligence been more essential to foreign and national security policy decisionmaking, formulation and planning than now, as we stand at the gates of a new century and a new millennium and face a future laden with unknowns. Further, our citizenry are playing a more important role and bringing greater influence to bear on the process of governance. For this reason, it is highly essential that they understand — to the extent that they can — the dynamics of relationships, cooperation and competition, in a modern world of nation-states, and that they strive to know the issues and take a stand on them. Teaching the basics of national intelligence to selected students in our colleges and universities is one way of helping to ensure that a vital segment of the *body publique* is at least partially informed.

PURPOSE OF PRESENTATION

Having said this, I would like to relate how one individual, an old, long-in-the-tooth "Huminter," endeavors to teach the subject of intelligence to a small, select group of undergraduate students. I ask you to remember while I talk that I have been at one part or another of the intelligence business for almost 60 years, beginning as point man for a rifle squad in 1940. I was introduced to problems of intelligence and guerrilla warfare with the Office of Strategic Services in 1942; I have fought behind enemy lines in WWII; I have worked as an intelligence staff officer, writing analyses and estimates; I have spotted, recruited, trained and dispatched paramilitary agents behind the Iron Curtain during the Cold War; I have conducted intricate and dangerous political action and grey and black propaganda programs for the Central Intelligence Agency during that same era; I have run spies, have served as a clandestine asset myself, have been surveilled for weeks at a time, have been arrested, detained, and I have been seduced — in the best interests of my country, of course. In short, I ask you to believe I know what the hell I am talking about.

CONCEPT OF LECTURE

My approach will be to cover the history and goals of a simple 15-week undergraduate course, entitled "An Overview of U.S. National Intelligence," to describe the structure and methodology employed and summarize learning outcomes.

BACKGROUND

The institution in question is Hampden-Sydney College in Southside, Virginia, the oldest men's college in the Nation and the 10th-oldest overall. Students in this particular

LTG Wilson presents Conference keynote address.

course are selected seniors with high grade point averages, some of them interested in intelligence as a possible career.

First, a word on how this particular academic endeavor evolved. I began teaching as an adjunct professor of Political Science at Hampden-Sydney several years after military retirement to my farm, located conveniently 12 miles from the College. My first course was somewhat pretentiously entitled "U.S. Foreign Policy and National Security 1982-2000: Threats, Issues and Responses." The teaching approach involved a rather large seminar (15-25 students), and the course was heavily over-subscribed from the beginning. I relied upon my own background as a primary resource, using anecdotes and illustrations from my experience in World War II and the Cold War as an intelligence officer, special operations practitioner and (reserve) Foreign Service officer. A significant segment of this initial course on foreign policy was quite logically devoted to U.S. foreign intelligence. Largely because of strong student interest, I expanded this intelligence segment into a separate, interdisciplinary course entitled "An Overview of U.S. National Intelligence." Both courses have attracted far more student interest than we have been able to accommodate.

I believe it is relevant for me to take a moment to tell you where I'm coming from and to show you at the same time how I endeavor to use stories to enliven and illustrate major teaching points. One way or the other, I have been involved in intelligence and related special operations since 1940-that's 59 years exactly, this June. I began my career in the old brown-shoe Army (Virginia National Guard) wearing wrapped leggings, the soldier's version of the Sam Browne belt and that old flat, WWI dishpan-shaped helmet. To my distress, I was initially assigned as the company bugler because of my musical background. It took me several months to work my way out of that job; I had first to recruit, then train my replacement. My early Christmas present in late fall 1940 was to be promoted to PFC and assigned as lead scout in a rifle squad. Anybody here ever have that nerve-wracking job?—rifle at high port in sweaty palms, creeping forward softly on the balls of your feet, eyes squinted sharply in all directions, ear balls straining for the slightest sound, watching squad leader out of the corner of one's eye for controlling signals and feedback ("collection guidance"), sniffing the wind for any unusual smells (and wondering if they emanate from your own sour, fear-induced sweat), and what is this signal? **Enemy in sight, over there." "A whole bunch of them"! This is indications and warning of the first order! The whole eight steps of the intelligence cycle, from requirements to feedback, represented in one man — one lonely, frightened man, a one-man intelligence agency — the lead scout in a rifle squad.

And from that I learned...

- The true importance of timely and effective indications and warning intelligence;
- That good intelligence operations always entail some calculated risk;
- That it is vital always to keep your eye on your customer; he's the reason you're there in the first place.

Then some 3 years later, I found myself in North Burma as a 19-year-old first lieutenant, intelligence and reconnaissance platoon leader — the point man — in essence, the chief reconnaissance officer, in the 5307th Composite Unit (Provisional), popularly known as "Merrill's Marauders." The initial challenge for the 3,000-man, all-volunteer light-infantry unit was to find a way to infiltrate into the enemy's rear area, to get well behind his front lines. While on a rather dicey deep patrol job to probe the Japanese tactical dispositions in the Hukawng Valley, I found a thinly patrolled gap and sneaked through it successfully. Unable to raise Merrill on the radio, I then left my men in place at a patrol base in enemy territory and returned on horseback some 30 miles at night back through enemy lines in the jungle to Merrill's command post to report my findings. Acting promptly on this intelligence, Merrill was thus enabled to force-march his entire command to a location deep in the enemy's rear and thus begin his very first engagement on highly favorable terms for the Marauders. This incident is said to mark the turning point of the Marauder's initial campaign. (I refer you to Charlton Ogburn Jr.'s *The Marauders* (New York: Harper and Brothers, 1959), 101-110.

And from that I learned...

- The importance of reporting intelligence in a timely manner;
- Again, that good intelligence operations always entail some calculated risk;
- That for intelligence to have real value, it must be acted on, sometimes quite promptly and decisively; otherwise, it can be about as useful as warm spit, regardless of how romantic or dramatic it may sound.

As an aside, I can trace my ultimately becoming a Foreign Area Officer and a specialist on the Soviet Union from the North Burma Campaign. During brief lulls in action — and there always are lulls in war — we would sometimes rig up our mule-packed radio (for some reason we called this radio "Becky") in a more wide-band listening mode, especially if we were high up in the mountains at night. By experimenting with the orientation of the antenna, we frequently could pick up major broadcasts from great distances, such as BBC, Radio Australia, Radio Calcutta, Japanese-sponsored Radio Free Rangoon, and on occasion strange-sounding newscasts of a program called "Govorit Moskva." One of my muleskinners, who was of Russian parentage, would interpret these Soviet battle communiques for me. Even the knowledge that these broadcasts were at least in part propaganda, designed to raise and maintain home-front morale, could not disguise the fact that on the Soviet-German Front the war was taking place on a scope and scale and creating a level of human devastation and suffering that we could hardly imagine where we were. It was then that I said to my little band that when the war was over, I intended to study Russian, go to

Moscow as an Army Attache Captain, and find out *why* these people were fighting and dying so bravely.

Slightly over three years later, in fall 1947, I entered Columbia University's Russian Institute as a member of the Army's Foreign Area Specialist Training Program/Russian (FAST-R, now FAOP/R) and launched my subsequent career as a Russian linguist and HUMINT specialist in Soviet affairs, a long, twisting, dangerous, sometimes hilarious, sometimes nightmarish, always fascinating 30-year trail that led through a bewildering variety of intelligence and special operations assignments and ultimately to the directorship of this Agency.

You may be beginning to wonder why I have gone into such detail concerning my own background. I have done so in order that you might perceive the extent to which my intelligence course today is deeply flavored and influenced by personal experience and subjective interpretations.

H-SC INDS 465:
"AN OVERVIEW OF U.S. NATIONAL INTELLIGENCE"

Now that we are finished with our brief historical excursions, let's look at the goals and methodology of the Hampden-Sydney College intelligence course itself, following which we will examine an outline summary of the course's highlights.

In essence, there are five basic objectives for this course:

- To provide an overall understanding of the U.S. National Foreign Intelligence institution and its activities;
- To help raise the level of individual student interest in current happenings of intelligence import and to assist in developing critical newsreading habits (to include using television and the Internet as a resource), especially where matters of U.S. foreign policy and national security are concerned;
- To provide an introduction to basic techniques involved in intelligence collection and analysis (pre-intelligence career course);
- To help the student further in learning how to apply individual reasoning faculties (problem solving);
- To give additional practice in oral and written presentations (intelligence briefing techniques).

As to structure and methodology, a deliberate effort is made to restrict the size of the class to a number conducive to the seminar approach, ideal size being about 15 students. The semester is broken down into 15 3-hour sessions, conducted once weekly in the evening. Significant emphasis is placed on practical work: Students are assigned real-world intelligence requirements, either as collectors or analysts. To carry out these tasks, they must make recourse to available daily, weekly, and monthly journals and news magazines, as well as to radio and television newscasts and to the Internet. Required readings are assigned for each session, most of them from Jeffrey T. Richelson's *The Intelligence*

Community. Each student is required to accomplish a book report, both orally and in writing, and there is a further requirement for a 10-page paper on an assigned intelligence topic to be rendered orally in class and then submitted to the instructor for review.

The chronological outline for the course itself breaks down as follows, using the course for Fall 1998 as a model:

An Overview of U.S. National Intelligence

"Intelligence is information plus analysis. Its primary purpose is helping the commander/policymaker to reach informed, reasoned and timely decisions and — above all — to avoid being surprised."

This course provides a basic overview of the history, current organization and missions of the U.S. National Foreign Intelligence establishment (the "Intelligence Community") and its various programs and activities in support of U.S. foreign policy and national security goals and objectives in the closing years of the 20th Century. Central themes include the critical need for sound and timely intelligence in the formulation and conduct of U.S. foreign policy and national security undertakings; the historical evolution of U.S. intelligence from colonial times to the present; principles for effective intelligence operations; moral and legal constraints imposed upon the intelligence institution in an open, democratic society; guidelines for preparing for a professional career in intelligence, with emphasis on the value of a broadly-based, liberal arts education. Extensive use is made of the case study approach for illustrative purposes. Each student is required to prepare and present an intelligence analysis on a potential threat to U.S. foreign policy interests.

Lecture Titles:

1. *An Introduction to Intelligence* (Give diagnostic test; collect biographic data; discuss syllabus) Introduction to intelligence as an institution, process, product, and profession; definitions, purpose, organizational principles; types and categories of intelligence; counterintelligence and counterespionage; security classifications; intelligence collection disciplines — SIGINT, IMINT/PHOTINT/HUMINT — and their subdisciplines; methods of evaluation; intelligence cycle.

2. *History of Intelligence* (Assign papers and book reports) A history of American intelligence from colonial times to the present, with emphasis on basic principles for effective intelligence and examples of recurring problems and issues.

3. *The U.S. Intelligence Institution.* The U.S. Intelligence Community — players and relationships; mechanisms for formulating intelligence policy and requirements, for coordinating collection operations and the estimative process; planning, programming and resource allocation.

4. *The Current World Setting.* A summary description of the foreign policy and national security world context within which today's intelligence activities take place.

5. *The Changing Face of War.* The evolving nature of human conflict from ancient times to the present with emphasis on the quantum leap effects of technological revolutions; comparisons of nuclear wars with conventional conflicts (World War II, Korea, the Gulf War), with revolutionary wars and "Wars of National Liberation" (Vietnam); characteristics of post-Cold War conflicts between cultures (Yugoslavia).

An Overview of U.S. National Intelligence (continued)

6. *U.S. Intelligence Collection Operations.* Nature and purpose of intelligence collection operations; Driving role of requirements in the collection process; handling the intelligence tasking process; particularized capabilities in the separate collection disciplines and their respective subdisciplines; HUMINT as the senior discipline — advantages and disadvantages; use of open sources in HUMINT; observers versus spies; role of attaches; clandestine and covert collection; types of agents; motivational considerations and recruitment techniques; principles and examples of clandestine tradecraft; technology in support of HUMINT.

7. *Intelligence Analyses and Estimates.* Role and functions of the intelligence analyst and the estimator; requisite skills, qualifications and personal characteristics of an effective analyst (if the collector is functional James Bond, then analysis is Sherlock Holmes); description of working environment; typical examples of problems and questions requiring analysis; processing — "bottleneck syndrome" between collection and analytical phases of intelligence cycle; intelligence estimates — purpose and process; estimative terminology; role of National Intelligence Council; historical examples of estimates. Separate squib on psychic research in the Soviet Union and the People's Republic of China as reported in open sources. Mid-term, take-home exam.

8. *Intelligence, Security, Counterintelligence (CI) and Covert Action.* Protecting intelligence; personnel, physical and document security; classification categories and procedures; Freedom of Information Act and policies for downgrading and release of intelligence; critical importance of protecting sources and methods. Counterintelligence — the "shadow world" of intelligence; definition of CI and listing of its four major functions; case histories involving KGB and U.S. services; moral issues. Separate brief examination of covert political action and covert paramilitary undertakings by U.S. clandestine services.

9. *Deception.* Definition, purposes, concepts, categories and levels of deception; case studies from history of successful deception operations; relationships between deception, psychological operations and covert action; roles of intelligence and special operations forces in deception; principles and guidelines for deception planning.

10. *Terrorism.* Primer on modern terrorism — definitions, goals and antecedents, tactics and techniques; factors influencing selection of targets by terrorists; influence and effects of technology (especially in weapons and explosives, as well as in transportation and communications); terrorist exploitation of public media; some do's and don'ts for counter-terrorist programs.

11. *Foreign Intelligence Services and Operations.* A descriptive survey of selected Allied and friendly intelligence organizations and consideration of the pluses and minuses of sharing intelligence; discussion of former Soviet intelligence services — KGB and GRU — their missions, characteristics and major activities and operations. Student book reports.

12. *Crisis Management.* Exercise; student book reports.

13. *Intelligence Policy and Management — Problems and Issues; Intelligence Oversight.* The dilemma of secret intelligence in a free society — secrecy in government versus the public's right to know, the costs of sensitive "leaks" to the public media; moral issues in intelligence — do the "ends justify the means?"; examples of intelligence excesses; do's and don'ts for effective oversight.

14. *Student Presentations.* Oral presentations covering intelligence analyses by separate students on selected subjects of current interest and relevance.

15. *Final Exam.* In class.

Every effort is expended to make the course interesting and lively. During the fall of 1991, students were assigned intelligence collection requirements and analytical responsibilities on the Persian Gulf. Because of the dynamics of that rapidly developing situation, they were able to determine very quickly for themselves whether their findings and prognoses had merit. The following year, to take advantage of the Presidential election in the fall of 1992, students were notionally identified as foreign intelligence officers and assigned in teams of five each in a number of foreign embassies in Washington (Russian, Chinese, British, French, German, Israeli, Japanese) and tasked to follow the progress of the campaign and provide political intelligence reporting back to the national intelligence directorates in their respective national capitals. I should note that, because of the strident student clamor to be enrolled in this particular class, I allowed it to swell in size to 35 students. I will not be doing this again.

And every lesson carries at least one war story, similar to the ones I used in the beginning of this presentation. Some of them are "pencils down" stories, like the references I am about to make.

As hinted earlier, I invested roughly 5 years in the late 1940s and early 1950s as an Army Captain and Major acquiring the Russian language and becoming a specialist on the Soviet Union. Three years of this period were spent as a student in Europe, involving not only intensive language and area studies but also a number of interesting extra-curricular diversions and special projects, such as serving as a part-time diplomatic courier and travelling in particular to and within the Soviet Union and throughout the Iron Curtain countries as well as visiting other countries on the periphery of the USSR. I also served as a liaison officer and in an escort officer capacity with elements of the Group of Soviet Forces in Eastern Austria, and later with the Group of Soviet Forces/Germany (GSFG), living, working and travelling with them.

And what did I learn from that? I have never learned so much in one period of time in my life.

- No matter how many books you read, lectures you attend, or papers you write, there is no substitute for being on the ground itself, walking the streets, seeing the sights, eating the food, rubbing elbows with the people, conversing, debating, arguing. That is why, years later, I set up the Analyst Travel Program in DIA. I did not want analysts to be writing about countries they had never seen.
- How little we know about how other people think!
- I also learned that while engaged in these activities I could be useful to some of our own operational intelligence friends by talking to them once in a while and finding out something about their priority interests and concerns. It is sometimes surprising how much you can see and hear and learn if you know what is important to look for. I didn't know it at the time, but I was setting myself up for some interesting future assignments.

By the mid-1950s I had already served a stint as a general staff officer in Army Intelligence in the Pentagon, a brief period as a consultant on Soviet affairs in the Pentagon, a similarly brief time on what is now the National Security Council staff, and was working as a Case Officer in the Clandestine Services of the Central Intelligence Agency. Clearly one of the most fascinating periods of my life.

West Berlin 1955-56 — a green island in a red sea, reminded me a little of the Marauders in North Burma and a patrol base deep in enemy territory, except this time it was much more complicated. By our count, there were 29 competing intelligence agencies in Berlin, all of them seemingly on opposite sides, snarling, growling, and working against each other — my first real encounter with the phenomenon of intelligence turf wars, this time in an international setting. Later I would encounter the same vicious bureaucratic in-fighting in Washington, only that would be major league stuff. In Berlin, we — the United States, the Brits, the French, and the West Germans spent so much time one-upping each other and stealing each other's operations that the Soviet GRU and the KGB had a field day. It was a wonder we ever got anything done of real intelligence value.

In my assignment the primary target was the GSFG and behind it the Soviet military in general. The requirements were many and difficult, and there were many and varied operational approaches. One of them for me included running a small platoon of ladies of the night (at one time 18 of them) with the priority target — the command structure of the GSFG. At times we had notable successes, the kind they write popular screen plays about; sometimes we had failures — and the failures were horrible. I still have nightmares.

And from that I learned:

- In intelligence discord is deadly, especially when you combine it with cut-throat competition.
- And when reminiscing about 18 brave, dedicated ladies of the night who were fighting the Cold War with the only weapon at their disposal and the successes they sometimes enjoyed, I am reminded that men are never so vulnerable as when they are in the grips of testosterone-driven passion.

CONCLUSION

Perhaps the most substantively important and topically relevant instructional unit of this entire course is the one that gets the shortest shrift. It pertains to intelligence policy and management, with primary emphasis on problems and issues, many of long standing, and to the vital function of intelligence oversight. Here we are talking about the dilemma posed by secret intelligence in a free society — secrecy in government versus the public's right to know, the costs of sensitive "leaks" to the public media; moral issues in intelligence — do the ends justify the means?; examples of intelligence excesses; do's and don'ts for effective intelligence oversight. This concluding unit of the course admittedly raises more questions than it answers, but it could well be that sensitizing young college students to intelligence quandaries that affect the long-term health and viability of the Republic is one of the most valuable outcomes of this academic undertaking.

Thank you. May I have your questions?

BIOGRAPHY
LTG Samuel V. Wilson, USA (Ret.)

Lieutenant General Samuel V. Wilson, a native of Southside Virginia, retired from active military service in 1977, having served during his 37-year career in every enlisted and commissioned rank from infantry Private to Lieutenant General. In addition to his World War II service described in this address, General Wilson's career highlights included a tour as an intelligence staff officer in the Pentagon, a CIA field case officer, a Special Forces Group Commander, Assistant for Special Operations, Assistant Division Command (Operations) of the 82nd Airborne Division, U.S. Defense Attache/Moscow, Deputy to the Director of Central Intelligence, and Director of DIA. Assignments to Vietnam were with the U.S. Agency for International Development as Associate Director for Field Operations, and subsequently in the U.S. Embassy as U.S. AID Mission Coordinator. In the latter position, he received a Presidential Appointment to the personal rank of Minister.

General Wilson is a graduate of the Infantry Officers Advanced Course, the Army Command and General Staff College and the Air War College. His decorations include the Distinguished Service Cross, Defense Distinguished Service Medal, Army Distinguished Service Medal with two Oak Leaf Clusters, National Intelligence Distinguished Service Medal, Silver Star with Oak Leaf Cluster, Legion of Merit with Oak Leaf Cluster, Bronze Star for Valor with Oak Leaf Cluster, Army Commendation Medal with two Oak Leaf Clusters, Purple Heart, Vietnamese Gallantry Cross with Palm, and the Vietnamese National Administration Medal for Exemplary Service.

Tighe Auditorium audience.

Mark Lowenthal, President and Chief Operating Officer of Open Source Solutions (USA), discusses papers from the morning session. At his right, Katherine Shelfer, Drexel University, and Mark Marshall, JMIC Faculty.

German liaison officer Colonel Klaus Euler visits with JMIC Academic Operations Dean John Robinson; Colonel Jurgen Eigenbrod, Commander, German Armed Forces Intelligence School; and Joint Military Intelligence College President A. Denis Clift.

TEACHING INTELLIGENCE:
WORKING TOGETHER TO BUILD A DISCIPLINE

Lloyd D. Salvetti
Director, Center for the Study of Intelligence
Central Intelligence Agency

A colleague told me that speaking here in the JMIC auditorium reminded him of the Dienbienphu school of architecture— "place the speaker on the low ground and fire down on him." Standing here, I understand the comparison.

Before we get started, I would like to poll you on the following question: How many of you were teaching an intelligence course in 1985? 1990? 1995? Today? We are making progress, but we have still some distance to go, in my view.

We have had a full morning of presentations and discussions. General Wilson's remarks on his experience in teaching intelligence created an excellent foundation for the rest of this morning's sessions, and the agenda for this afternoon promises to be stimulating as well. I hope I can contribute to the dialogue.

I want to compliment Denis Clift, President of the Joint Military Intelligence College, for organizing this event. The last conference of this sort, of which I am aware — occurred in 1993 and was sponsored by the institution I represent, CIA's Center for the Study of Intelligence. I think we ought to have such a conference about every five years to take a measure of how we are doing, and what we must do to enhance this particular niche of academic research, writing and teaching.

I know that we have participants from several nations at this conference. They enrich the quality of the dialogue on teaching intelligence for all of us. We need to increase the representation of foreign scholars and teachers at these conferences. Debate, discussion, research, and writing on the history, practice, and the proper role of intelligence in a democracy should be promoted in every way possible. To underscore this point, we practitioners in this country need to heed the words of former Director of Central Intelligence, the late William Colby, who in his 1978 memoir wrote:

> Whatever may have been the tradition of the past, [i]t is... essential that the relationship of the people to our intelligence apparatus be redefined and made appropriate to modern America... Intelligence must accept the end of its special status in the American government, and take on the task of informing the public of its nature and its activities as any other department or agency. ...Thus, the public must be informed of what intelligence is doing in its name and how this contributes to the general welfare of the Nation. Excerpt from: *Honorable Men: My Life in the CIA* (New York: Simon and Schuster, 1978), 459-460.

I believe the intent of his reflection on the importance of communicating to the American public the purpose and role of intelligence in the American system of government applies equally to the need to foster and support the teaching of intelligence at U.S. academic institutions. Moreover, we ought to promote and support the debate, discussion, research, and writing on the history, practice and the proper role of intelligence in a democracy in other countries. Inviting foreign scholars and representatives of foreign governments to conferences of this sort is an important step in that direction. We in the Center for the Study of intelligence welcome opportunities to support and collaborate with academic institutions and think tanks in the U.S. and overseas interested in sponsoring such conferences.

As you have heard, I am a practitioner of the craft of intelligence, having served in positions ranging from intelligence collector to intelligence analyst to intelligence consumer. I am a career operations officer who took over the helm at the Center in October of last year. I have served in the United States and overseas, in a variety of senior management position in CIA, and in policy support positions. My practitioner experience has been in two areas: intelligence collection operations and covert action — the latter including the design and operational control of some of the larger covert action programs of the Reagan years in Washington and in managing the policy process of covert action in President Bush's NSC. I have taught and continue to teach intelligence at the National War College and I have lectured on intelligence at various universities. It is from that perspective that I welcome the opportunity to discuss teaching the American system of intelligence with you.

Before I do that, however, I would like to acquaint you with CSI in the hope that we can become a resource for those of you teaching about the craft of intelligence. For those of you unfamiliar with CSI, we are essentially the Agency's "think tank" on intelligence issues. In this capacity:

- We produce the classified and unclassified history of CIA — the CIA History Staff is in CSI;
- We support the State Department's production of the *Foreign Relations of the United States* volumes;
- We sponsor and conduct classified and unclassified research on intelligence programs and activities by active duty and retired Agency officers;
- We publish *Studies in Intelligence* — the journal of record of the intelligence profession;
- We write and publish books and monographs;
- We host conferences and symposia; and,
- We coordinate several academic outreach programs and activities.

I hope some of you are familiar with our recent work. Let me cite a few examples:

- Last September, CSI hosted, in collaboration with the U.S. Air Force, the National Reconnaissance Office, and three aerospace firms (Lockheed-Martin, Raytheon, and Kodak) a very successful conference on the past, present and future of the U-2 program. As part of the conference, we published *The CIA and the U-2 Program*,

1954-1974, the CIA's now -declassified internal history of the U-2 program. It is the only history of the program based upon both full access to CIA records and extensive classified interviews with many of its participants.

■ In 1996, we organized, in cooperation with the National Security Agency, the Venona conference and published concomitantly the volume, *Venona: Soviet Espionage and the American Response, 1939-1957*. As you know, Venona was the codeword for the program that sought to read and exploit Soviet intelligence messages collected in the 1940s. The book contains important declassified U.S. Government documents outlining the U.S. response to Soviet espionage, as well as 99 of the most significant and revealing Soviet messages translated by Western analysts.

This year we are sponsoring two additional conferences:

■ In September, we will collaborate with the German Allied Museum on our first overseas conference, to be held in Berlin. The conference, entitled "Berlin: The Intelligence War (1946-1961)," will bring together Cold War intelligence veterans from both sides of the Iron curtain, academics, and authors to discuss the intelligence dimensions of some of the pivotal events of the early Cold War, from the Berlin Blockade to the famous tank standoff at checkpoint Charlie in 1961.

■ We also have begun organizing for a conference in collaboration with the George Bush School of Government and Public Service, and the Center for Presidential Studies at Texas A&M University on the "Role of Intelligence in the End of the Cold War." President George Bush will participate in several events at the conference, as will former Secretary of State James Baker, former Secretary of Defense Richard Cheney, former Advisor to the President for National Security Affairs Brent Scowcroft, and former DCI Judge William Webster. Former DCI and Assistant to the President Bob Gates will be the keynote speaker. For release at the conference, we are preparing a collection of declassified national intelligence estimates on the Soviet Union and Eastern Europe that were written during the closing months of the Cold War and the collapse of Communism in the Soviet Union.

Let me also mention some of the books our Center has recently published:

■ Earlier this year, The Society for History in the Federal Government bestowed one of its most prestigious awards, the George Pendleton Prize for the best major manuscript on a U.S. Government program, on a book CSI published: *CIA and the Vietnam Policymakers* by Hal Ford. The book is a candid and scholarly account of how the U.S. Intelligence Community, particularly the CIA, provided wartime intelligence support to the Kennedy and Johnson Administrations — and how U.S. policymakers, at times, brought great pressure to bear on analysts to treat controversial aspects of the problem in ways more favorable to Administration war aims and how analysts resisted the pressure. More often than not the CIA got it right in Vietnam.

■ Our newest book is by Doug MacEachin, a former CIA Deputy Director for Intelligence, who has written *The Final Months of the War with Japan: Signals Intelligence, U.S. Invasion Planning, and the A-Bomb Decision.* This book uses newly discovered, declassified SIGINT to show that the Japanese were dramatically expanding their defensive forces in the area chosen as the invasion point on the Japanese home islands by U.S. planners, thereby likely ensuring heavy U.S. casualties if an invasion had taken place.

■ Let me also say a word about our journal, *Studies in Intelligence.* It has been published since 1955, but the first unclassified edition did not appear until 1992. The publication is the U.S. Government's journal of the intelligence profession. Our objective in publishing *Studies in Intelligence* is to capture historical, operational, or doctrinal aspects of intelligence for students of the intelligence profession (unclassified edition) and for practitioners (the classified edition). I believe *Studies* would be a valuable resource for teachers and students about various intelligence issues. For example, the latest unclassified issue carries articles on such subjects as:

■ "Calling the Sino-Soviet Split: The CIA and Double Demonology," which chronicles the debate within the Intelligence Community on the nature of the Sino-Soviet relationship to 1963, by which time the estrangement had become public.

■ "Planning Satellite Reconnaissance to Support Military Operations," an article proposing a new doctrine for reconnaissance operations.

All of these materials and more are available to you as intelligence scholars. I have brought copies of the latest issues of the unclassified *Studies* and other unclassified materials published by CSI for those of you desiring a copy. They are on a table at the entrance to the Conference Hall for you to pick up at the end of the session. If you do not now receive our publications, please complete one of the forms on the publications table and we will add you to our mailing list. You can also gain access to our unclassified materials on the CSI home page on the CIA Internet site. Additionally, next year we are committed to producing a compendium of intelligence course syllabi, and we invite each of you to submit yours for inclusion in this publication. We also want to serve as a bridge between you and the rest of the CIA, locating speakers for you, placing your students in touch with our recruiters, and so on. Finally, I urge you to invite CSI officers, especially our historians, to lecture in your classes and participate in your seminars and colloquia.

Let me just say a few words about our History Staff. It consists of six superb historians led by Gerry Haines, the CIA Chief Historian. They produce a steady stream of classified and unclassified monographs, articles, and books, which are consistently recognized for the quality of their scholarship and writing. Our historians hold PhDs in history or political science, have extensive "line" experience within the Agency, as analysts or operations officers, and are experienced lecturers.

To underscore the unique role played by CIA historians, I am pleased to announce that we have recently begun a program that will help us capture more fully the history of CIA: a systematic oral history program. We understand, of course, that not every historian is an enthusiastic supporter of oral history. But in our organization, in particular, in which the details of sensitive operations are frequently captured in a variety of documents with limited dissemination or even not written down, as was the practice in some of the most sensitive operations in the 1950s, we think an oral history program will make an important contribution to our understanding of history and the evolution of the intelligence profession.

So that is my offer to you. If you are teaching a course on intelligence and would like our support, be it in securing copies of our publications or in requesting a guest speaker, call us. We will do everything we can to help you. We would like to be your guide to unclassified and declassified resources in CIA and the rest of the Intelligence Community that might benefit you in your courses.

What can we bring to the table? To answer that question, let me quote something Professor Ernest May of Harvard's John F. Kennedy school said at a CIA-sponsored symposium on teaching intelligence earlier this decade:

> Access to documents is only part of what scholars need from the Intelligence Community. ... Scholars need orientation to the world from which the documents emerge so they can understand and evaluate the documents, make informed guesses about the extent to which the essential record is complete or incomplete, and cross-question memoirs and testimony.

To illustrate his point, May related the following anecdote:

> Some years ago, an eminent and exceedingly able scholar presented at the Woodrow Wilson Center a paper dealing with postwar planning during World War II by the Joint Chiefs of Staff. (JCS) The paper made much of some memoranda issuing from a JCS committee composed of very senior officers. General Andrew Goodpaster [Eisenhower's personal secretary] commented on the paper. Though with characteristic tact, General Goodpaster made the point that those particular senior officers were not ones in whose judgment the Chiefs of Staff placed great trust. 'If you are looking for the memoranda to which General Marshall paid attention,' General Goodpaster said, 'find those with the initials GAL for Col. George A. Lincoln. That was the person Marshall respected.'

> The basic point is one that any academic should appreciate. ... To thread one's way through the immense volume of papers in any modern government agency, scholars need the kind of guidance that General Goodpaster offered — about whose initials mattered to whom. That information has to come from people who where there.

— From *Symposium on Teaching Intelligence: October 1-2, 1993 (Washington, DC: CSI, April 1994), 7-8.*

My point is: *Let us be your guide.* We want to be a resource to you.

To facilitate communications between you and the Center, I have named Dr. John Hedley to be CSI's Academic Referent. John just recently retired after a distinguished 33-year career with the Agency. Among his many important assignments, John taught a graduate course on intelligence and wrote several articles for academic journals from 1993 to 1995. He continues to teach intelligence courses at Georgetown, and is on the editorial board of the *International Journal of Intelligence and CounterIntelligence.* I would like John to be in frequent correspondence with you — via the telephone, the Internet or the post office. I would like to see him making visits to your campuses to observe and participate in your courses and seminars. I hope you will view him as *your* resource.

I am sure some of you will be asking yourselves, "Why? Why is he proposing this?" I can assure you that it is not because we want to put a pro-CIA spin on intelligence history. I can assure you that our historians are ready, willing and able to call them as they see them. They have no need to fear for their careers when they produce works that are critical of the Agency.

No, I want to help you because I believe it is important. It is important that the public be given a realistic and historically accurate picture of the intelligence profession — its successes and its failures; its strengths and its weaknesses. It is no longer adequate to have the history of intelligence written by journalists and malcontents. It is no longer acceptable to have an intelligence agency, or the Intelligence Community as a whole, unnecessarily or inappropriately isolated from the citizens from whom it draws its funding, its recruits, its political support — indeed for whom it works.

If I may quote former DCI Bob Gates,

The purpose of greater openness is to make CIA and the intelligence process more visible and understandable. We must try to help people understand better what CIA does and how we do it. Our... approach grows out of the belief that it is important that CIA should be accountable to the American people — both directly and through the Congress — as a law-abiding organization [comprising] talented people of integrity who have a critical role in supporting national security policymakers in a complex and often dangerous world. We are under no illusions that CIA, whatever the level of its efforts, will be able to win recognition as an 'open' institution. What we hope to do is all we can do to be as forthcoming, candid, informative, and helpful as possible to the public, the media, and academia consistent with our mission and the protection of sources and methods.

— From "CIA and Openness," address by DCI Gates to Oklahoma Press Association, 21 February 1992.

In my view, the time is well past for moving public knowledge of the intelligence profession beyond the image it has received in countless pieces of pulp fiction and Hollywood adventure movies, in which intelligence professionals are regularly either demonized or treated as omniscient and omnipotent superheroes. No one who bases his understanding of intelligence on *The Hunt for Red October,* for example, would have the slightest idea what role an intelligence analyst plays, or how the intelligence process as a whole works, for that matter.

In fact, our experience has been that even many experienced military officers and civilian employees in national security agencies frequently have a limited understanding of what we do or how we do it. To help remedy that situation, I believe we need to explore creation of a National Intelligence University that would more fully inform professional military officers and civilian government employees about the capabilities and processes of the Intelligence Community. Our University would not necessarily have a campus, but rather would consist of coordinated course offerings that would be taught by the Intelligence Community members. For example, NSA could offer a course on SIGINT collection and analysis; CIA could teach HUMINT collection; NRO and the National Imagery and Mapping Agency could teach imagery; DIA could offer a course on military and tactical intelligence and so on. The model for such a National Intelligence University is right in this building. I believe the Joint Military Intelligence College is the foundation for such a university.

Similarly, I believe the way to close the gap between intelligence professionals and the citizens they work for is to promote the serious academic study of, and research into, the intelligence profession. I think many of you would agree that courses on intelligence are badly underrepresented at American universities. We can all list our favorite reasons for that. Some might point out that it is for the same reason that such subjects as military history are underrepresented: such courses are simply out of favor in the prevailing sociopolitical climate on campuses and within disciplines today. Some might mention the James Bond syndrome as a cause: the derring-do of secret agents surely can't be seriously discussed as an academic topic. Some might point out that intelligence studies have largely been captured by the larger field of diplomatic history, where the tendency seems to be to treat intelligence as a minor sideshow whose contributions have been largely unimportant in the vast sweep of the foreign policy process. There is, however, another, important reason that I am sure many of you are thinking about.

I suspect many of you might mention the limited availability of source material as a reason for the lack of courses on intelligence. After all, you can't teach it if you can't first research it. And you can't research it if the source material isn't available. Perhaps just as importantly, if you can see only some of the material on a given subject and not all of it, how can you trust what you see? The matter of mistrust looms large in all this, and it is focused on the CIA much more so than on any other government agency involved in intelligence activities.

At this point, the "D" word stares us right in the face: *DECLASSIFICATION!* Is the CIA doing all that it could to declassify records, the release of which would no longer harm the national security? Before going any further let me hasten to note that I am not in charge of the Agency's declassification programs. But I can say a few words about DCI George Tenet's commitment to declassification.

In July 1998, he issued a statement on declassification that reads in part as follows:

Although much of our work must be done in secrecy, we have a responsibility to the American people, and to history, to account for our actions and the quality of our work. Accordingly, I have made a serious commitment to the public release of information that with the passage of time no longer needs to be protected under our security classification system. *http://www.odci.gov/cia/public_affairs/ press_release/archives/1998/ps071598.html*

To achieve his declassification goals, little more than a year ago, the DCI created the Office of Information Management (OIM) to consolidate the operations and management of the various information review and release functions at CIA. During this brief period of time, OIM has made substantial progress in meeting the demands of the public and complying with a multitude of legislative mandates. Let me mention just a few of our accomplishments last year:

- CIA released more than one million pages of records under the 25-year declassification requirements of Executive Order 12958. This year, we expect to review five million pages, and eight million or more pages a year thereafter.
- We closed in excess of 7,000 Freedom of Information Act (FOIA)/Privacy Act (PA) requests, 2,000 more cases than the prior year and a record for the program, which began in 1975. As a result, we were able to reduce the backlog of FOIA/ PA requests by over 1,000 cases — a drop of about 20 percent.
- We reviewed for classified information and approved in a timely manner more than 300 manuscripts — over 20,000 pages — by current and former employees for publication in newspapers, books, journals, and the like.
- We released well over 200,000 pages of JFK assassination records in full compliance with federal legislation mandating the review and release of these materials.

Having cited those statistics, let me quote again from DCI Tenet's July 1998 statement:

None of this is easy. There are no shortcuts here. It takes experienced, knowledgeable people sitting down with each document and going over it page by page, line by line. There is no alternative. We take our obligation to protect those who have worked with us in the past very seriously. We also have to consider the impact of release on our ongoing diplomatic and intelligence relationships. A mistake on our part can put a life in danger or jeopardize a bilateral relationship integral to our security.

Suffice it to say, the demands for declassification review far exceed the capabilities of the personnel who are available under current budgetary limitations to perform it. This forces us to make choices in terms of what information will be reviewed first. In setting these priorities, the Agency is guided by its responsibilities under the law and Executive Order, as well as by policies established by the DCI.

In fact, CIA now has the equivalent of over 350 people working full time declassifying documents. I can assure you that this number compares very favorably to the number of employees the Agency has assigned to several of its most important core missions.

I would also like to express my hope that our greater openness in recent years has contributed to the expansion of intelligence literature that has taken place in the last few years. In 1994-95, there were only 215 intelligence books listed in *Books in Print*; today, there are 813. There is a great deal of material publicly available to support courses in intelligence, material to support research and writing on all the elements of the intelligence profession, and material available to write new books on all aspects of intelligence.

I do not imagine that this will satisfy those of you who are suspicious of us or those who are simply impatient with us. Nor do I want to give the impression that I am saying, "Trust us." I only want to emphasize that I personally believe the CIA and DCI George Tenet have a serious commitment to declassifying and releasing documents, consistent with our mission responsibilities, just as quickly as possible.

My objective is to communicate that we are trying to do the right thing. But it would be disingenuous of me to stand here and try to use these data to infer that the dam on the release of the full range of intelligence documents — operational cables, source files, the detail of espionage operations and similar documentation will be breached. Analytical products that deal with the gamut of issues addressed by CIA and the Intelligence Community will be declassified *unless* in their declassification we endanger a source, expose a method, or have the potential to seriously damage our relations with a foreign government.

At the end of the day, the choice for us is clear — as is required by law and our conscience — we are going to protect those men and women who choose to secretly work for the U.S. Government against terrorists, rogue states, proliferators of mass destruction weapons and anyone else who seeks to harm U.S. citizens or U.S. interests.

Earlier, I tried to answer the question: Why is he proposing this? There is another reason I feel strongly it is important to study the history and role of U.S. intelligence. There are 77 stars inscribed on the wall at CIA Headquarters for the men and women who gave their last full measure of devotion to their country. Of those 77 stars, 38 are not identified because they died in secrecy, under cover, anonymous to the world but heroes to those of us privileged to have served with them. They sought to protect America and Americans from those who threatened our freedoms and our way of life. We owe it to them to study the profession in which they served their country and to tell their story as fully and completely as possible.

Let me turn now to some other steps the Center is taking to promote the teaching and study of intelligence in our universities.

Many of you will be familiar with our Officer in Residence Program, in which we sponsor CIA offices for two-year tours on the faculties of participating colleges and universities, such as we did with John Hedley at Georgetown. The CIA officers are visiting faculty members. They teach, conduct research, and act as a resource for faculty colleagues and students. Each assignment is tailored to the individual and the institution. Many Offices-in-Residence speak to community groups and lecture at other, nearby academic institutions as well.

Second, I believe we need to do more to promote research and writing on intelligence topics at the undergraduate and graduate levels. To promote such research and writing, I would like to announce here that the Center is creating an annual award, which will be presented to the undergraduate or graduate student who writes the best essay on an intelligence topic at an American university. The competition will be judged by the editorial board of *Studies in Intelligence*, and the winning paper each year will be published in *Studies*.

Third, CIA sponsors the Harvard University Intelligence and Policy Project, which supports research and training on how intelligence is actually used, or not used, by government officials devising national security policies. The research culminates in the preparation of case studies on particular policy episodes. The project was founded in 1987 to help those who prepare assessments of foreign events, and those who make foreign policy decisions, better understand one another's needs, interests, cultures and perspectives. The program has produced 18 case studies, on such topics as *The SS-9 Controversy: Intelligence as Political Football, The Fall of the Shah of Iran*, and *The CIA and the Fall of the Soviet Empire: The Politics of 'Getting It Right'*. We hope you make use of these cases and the new cases that will be written with our support.

Finally, I would like to point to the compendiums of declassified documents with historical commentary that we produce in conjunction with our conferences. These unique volumes make fine starting points for professors seeking source material for courses on the Agency or the intelligence profession. In addition to the volumes I mentioned earlier, let me mention several others that are available to you:

- *The CIA under Harry Truman;*
- *Assessing the Soviet Threat: The Early Cold War Years;*
- *Corona: America's First Satellite Program;*

These volumes combine an interpretive historical essay with selective, representative declassified documents.

So what should we be teaching in our courses on intelligence? I'm sure each of you has your own strongly held views on this subject which I hope you will share with me in the course of this conference, but I thought I might close out my presentation here today by giving you a summary of the major themes I think are important in understanding the intelligence process today. These are in no particular order.

- *First, the growth in importance of technology, especially technical means of collection.* In the mid-1950s, perhaps the most important event in the history of American intelligence took place: the joining of government (in the form of the CIA and the Air Force), academia (in the person of such intellectual giants as James Killian of MIT), and business (Lockheed, Kodak, Polaroid, etc.) to produce the technical systems that finally allowed the U.S. to keep tabs on the strategic threat from the Soviet Union, which had proven largely impervious to the classical methods of HUMINT. The question for today, it seems to me, "Can this triumvirate, which is already strained, continue to provide the United States with technological superiority in the intelligence field?"

- *Second, the growth of oversight, especially Congressional oversight, but also more generally, public scrutiny as evidenced by the far more intensive press coverage that intelligence activities receive, closer attention from the Executive Branch, and also from the Judiciary.* It would be hard for me to exaggerate the sea-change the Congressional investigation of the 1970s and the subsequent formation of the oversight committees caused in the Agency's culture and practices. As some of you may know, there were occasions in the 1950s when the Congress would pass the Agency's budget without even holding hearings on it, and one or two powerful Senators and Representatives, such as Richard Russell and Clarence Cannon, would carefully limit the access of other members of Congress to Agency briefings. The change in the relationship is illustrated in the following statistic: Last year, Agency officers briefed members or staffers on 1,350 occasions, or an average of five times per working day.

- *Third, the influence of intelligence on policy, and concomitantly, the influence of politics and policymakers on intelligence.* What has been the impact of intelligence in the broader foreign policy formulation process? Under what circumstances do policymakers use intelligence? Ignore intelligence? Try to influence intelligence? What causes certain Presidents, like John Kennedy, to regularly read intelligence, and others, like Lyndon Johnson, to remain almost completely uninterested?

And does it matter? Sherman Kent, the Chairman of the Board of National Estimates from 1952 to 1967, once famously said,

> A certain amount of all this worrying we do about influence upon policy is off the mark. For in many cases, no matter what we tell the policymakers, and no matter how right we are and how convincing, he will upon occasion disregard the thrust of our findings for reasons beyond our ken. If influence cannot be our goal, what should it be? Two things. It should be relevant within the area of our competence, and above all it should be credible.

Is, therefore, the search for signs of influence a feckless endeavor? Kent himself came to the conclusion that, "In the last analysis, if the [National Intelligence Estimates] did nothing else, they contributed to a higher level of discourse in matters affecting the security of the country."

- *A fourth theme is the importance of the DCI as leader, administrator, and intelligence advisor to the President.* What makes a successful DCI? Which DCIs have been successful and why? George Tenet is the fifth DCI to lead CIA and the Intelligence Community in this decade. The average tenure of DCIs in the 1990s has been about 19 months, and given the many and lengthy nomination and confirmation processes for all the DCI nominees, the Agency was without a DCI for more than one year of the last nine years. What has caused this trend, and what will be its impact? Can it continue in the future without doing great harm to the Agency, the Community, and the Nation?

- *Fifth, the use of covert action by administrations through history.* How have U.S. presidents used covert action as an instrument of statecraft since the founding of the republic? What was the role of covert action during the Cold War? Was it a surrogate for conflict between military forces of the United States and the Soviet Union? Was it a "quick fix" for problems administrations could not otherwise solve? How important has covert action been as a policy tool? And what are the costs to the Agency for undertaking politically unpopular covert actions at presidential direction?

- *Sixth, the relevancy of secret intelligence in the Information Age.* Have the classical methods of intelligence collection, analysis, and dissemination been made nearly obsolete by the multiplicity of information sources that policymakers now have at their disposal? What role is left for these traditional methods? What contributions have they made in the past, and does the velocity at which information moves today make it possible for them to make similar contributions in the future? Can intelligence be used to harness the promise of the Information Age?

- *Another theme could be the partnership of intelligence with law enforcement and the military.* What is the proper relationship between law enforcement and intelligence? How closely should CIA and the FBI collaborate in their respective missions? What should be the role of intelligence and the military in addressing such transnational issues as counternarcotics, counterterrorism, and international organized crime?

- *Eighth, the fundamental question of the role of a secret intelligence organization in a democratic society.* What should be the role of CIA in the new millennium? In what circumstances should we conduct espionage? What is the ethical basis for espionage? What are the ethical challenges in producing all-source analysis for policymakers?

- *Finally, successes and failures.* The most important question of all: Have the American people gotten their money's worth out of the Intelligence Community? Just what is an "intelligence failure?" Are things simply right or wrong in the intelligence business? Or is success measured more accurately along a continuum, in which we should strive to be mostly right most of the time? Is perfect knowledge possible?

I am sure many of you could come up with an equally interesting list just as long as this one, and that is why I want to urge you to submit your syllabus to us for inclusion in the compendium of intelligence syllabi that we intend to produce next year. We can all learn from each other.

In conclusion, I would like to suggest that we can form a very successful partnership to advance the study of intelligence in our universities. I hope that I have been able to convince you of our genuine commitment to this goal. I have tried to outline for you what we are doing to foster the growth of intelligence studies at present and what we plan to do in the near future. I have even, perhaps somewhat presumptuously, suggested some of the themes we think it is important to address in classes on intelligence.

Rest assured, we will be "out there," lecturing, discussing, and presenting papers about intelligence. But in the end, there are many more of you than there are of us, and it is you and your colleagues who are in the best position to advance the field from its present status as something of a curiosity taught in a relative handful of universities to a more broadly accepted academic subject that will be offered as a standard part of most universities' curricula. It is you who will have to endow it with the conceptual and theoretical framework that will give the subject greater academic legitimacy. It is you who will have to attract the students, you who will have to do the research, write the papers, organize the conferences, and do the dozens of other things that will be required to ensure that the study of intelligence grows as a legitimate field of study.

We at the Center for the Study of Intelligence stand ready to help you. Together, I am confident we can do it.

BIOGRAPHY
Lloyd D. Salvetti

Mr. Lloyd D. Salvetti was appointed Director of CIA's Center for the Study of Intelligence in August 1998, following a tour of duty at the National War College, where he was a faculty member in the Department of National Security Policy. A veteran CIA operations officer, Mr. Salvetti has served in a variety of commands and other positions both abroad and domestically, including senior management posts in the Operations Directorate. Prior to his National War College assignment, he was Chief of Staff for the Deputy Director for Operations.

Mr. Salvetti served in 1989-1990 as Director of Intelligence Programs on the National Security Council staff. Before joining CIA in 1970, he managed a congressional office for two years. He was an active duty officer in the U.S. Air Force for four years in the 1960s, after which he served in intelligence positions as an Air Force Reservist. Mr. Salvetti received a B.A. from Tufts University and did postgraduate work at George Washington University, American University, and the Harvard Business School.

Panel on academic and Intelligence Community competitive assessments: Discussant H. Bradford Westerfield, Yale University; Davis Bobrow and Michael Rattie, University of Pittsburgh; and moderator Robert Mirabello, JMIC Faculty Member.

JMIC Faculty Member Perry Pickert
introduces the panel on United Nations
online documentation.

Panel on United Nations documents: Ms. Lilia Vazquez, David Traystman, LtCol Peter Vercruysse
(USMC) and Dr. H. Bradford Westerfield, Discussant.

CLOSING REMARKS

Dr. Ronald D. Garst
Provost, Joint Military Intelligence College

Our discussions today lead me to the conclusion that the teaching of intelligence has reached a new level of maturity. At one time, many of the course offerings on intelligence focused on the flashy part of the business — counterintelligence and covert operations. Today, those teaching intelligence generally avoid the sensational and focus on the role of intelligence in the national security of the United States and more broadly, global security. I am pleased to see a growing number of professors, proud of their association with the Intelligence Community, aiming their courses at those young people who wish to pursue careers in intelligence. In doing so, they are offering academic excellence with practical experience.

Teaching is facilitated by a growing body of intelligence literature. Serious scholars of intelligence, many of them with experience in the Intelligence Community, are writing about the activity and products of intelligence in an insightful and responsible manner. The dialog that started 50 years ago, in 1949, with the publication of Sherman Kent's *Strategic Intelligence for American World Policy,* continues today with Mark Lowenthal's soon-to-be-published *Intelligence: From Secrets to Policy.* Thanks to those in our midst who have been willing to put pen-to-paper, or in this cyber era, fingers-to-the-keyboard, professors have the factual, thoughtful and discerning material needed to teach intelligence to those who might aspire to join us. To those who today have shared their syllabi, teaching methods and lessons learned, we are grateful for your ideas.

Lloyd Salvetti noted that the JMIC is already the *de facto* core of a National Intelligence College or University. Let me suggest that, just as public schools often become the glue that holds today's diverse communities together, so can this College become the prime mover in orchestrating the evolution toward a more well-integrated Intelligence Community. For example, the new Occasional Paper by recent MSSI graduate Lisa Krizan, *Intelligence Essentials for Everyone,* melds together diverse views on the government intelligence cycle and further, in the spirit of openness fostered by an academic institution within the Community, extends her findings to those in the Nation's private sector businesses who have an interest in the principles and practices of information management for the security of their own operations.

This morning both Mark Marshall and Katherine Shelfer invited us to see some aspects of the intelligence business in a more revealing way than usual. We all took a step toward a deeper understanding of intelligence production based on the visual arts, and of the intricacies of tradeoffs between timeliness and accuracy in business information management, in the world of competitive intelligence. This afternoon, the issue of whether and how to structure tests of competing teams of "inside" and "outside" estimative analysts brought some sharp debate and some thoughtful rebuttals.

27

The team that just now brought us the story of how the United Nations is making even its draft documents available for academic debate by scholars-in-formation in the world's classrooms illustrates that linkages are becoming quite common between institutions that create public policy and those of us anywhere who can help provide informed debate. That is to say, the voices of well-informed individuals, mediated through group discussion, are being welcomed in at least some policy circles. When we realize that these voices are adding value to information, the worlds of academicians, intelligence analysts, and public officials acting on our behalf will be approaching a "meeting of the minds" in a way similar to what we have experienced here today.

During this conference I have witnessed a number of exchanges of business cards and e-mail addresses. As people get to know each other, I am sure the Internet will facilitate increased collaboration and cooperation in the teaching of intelligence. This is important for I suspect that many of you feel like lone wolves — teaching in an area little known by your colleagues, and viewed with suspicion by many. I urge you to persist. Invite the skeptics to your classes. They too will learn that this is an important, serious and extraordinarily interesting business.

In 1993 the CIA's Center for the Study of Intelligence hosted a symposium on the release of material essential to understanding the role of intelligence in U.S. policymaking. Today the College has sponsored a conference on the teaching of intelligence. Sometime in the middle years of the next decade, if not before, we trust some organization will host another conference such as this so that we may have another benchmark of our progress.